PRAISE FOR

# Faith Begins @ Home
# DEVOTIONS

Nothing strikes fear in the heart of a parent like the phrase "family devotions." But Mark Holmen shows us that this critical faith-building practice doesn't have to be a struggle; it's a privilege and a blessing that can be exciting, enriching and engaging for parents and kids alike.

## Jim Daly
President and CEO, Focus on the Family

As a senior pastor, Mark Holmen demonstrated how a local church can inspire and equip families to instill strong faith in the next generation. As a partner in the Strong Families Innovation Alliance, he has also been a mentor to other leaders trying to turn the tide of declining generational faith transference.

## Kurt Bruner
Executive Director, Strong Families Innovation Alliance

Mark Holmen is energizing families to grow their faith in the home. Mark and his message is one of the freshest and most practical voices among Christian leaders. This resource is helping us follow the mandate of God to pass on our faith from generation to generation.

## Jim Burns, Ph.D.
President, HomeWord
Senior Director of the Center for Youth and Family at Azusa Pacific University

Mark Holmen clearly knows what spiritual development in the family should look like, and he knows how to communicate that message in a warm, transparent and engaging way. Parents who digest the four Faith Begins @ Home booklets will have their vision lifted, their hearts warmed, and their minds focused on the practical things they can do to see their children embrace Christ for a lifetime. I recommend these resources to every believing family.

## Richard Ross, Ph.D.
Professor of Student Ministry at Southwestern Seminary
Fort Worth, Texas

Mark Holmen is providing much-needed leadership in the Faith@Home movement that is sweeping our nation. These resources are excellent tools in that they both challenge and equip parents as they seek to disciple their own children.

## Steve Stroope
Lead Pastor, Lake Pointe Church
Rockwall, Texas

# Mark Holmen

Author, *Faith Begins at Home* and Founder of Faith @ Home Ministries

# Faith Begins
# @Home
# DEVOTIONS

**Regal**

From Gospel Light
Ventura, California, U.S.A.

Published by Regal
From Gospel Light
Ventura, California, U.S.A.
*www.regalbooks.com*
Printed in the U.S.A.

Library of Congress Cataloging-in-Publication Data
Holmen, Mark.
Faith begins @ home devotions / Mark Holmen.
p. cm.
ISBN 978-0-8307-5229-4 (trade paper)
1. Families—Religious life. I. Title.
II. Title: Faith at home devotions.
BV4526.3.H66 2010
248.8'45—dc22
2009046384

1 2 3 4 5 6 7 8 9 10 / 16 15 14 13 12 11 10

Rights for publishing this book outside the U.S.A. or in
non-English languages are administered by Gospel Light Worldwide, an international not-for-profit ministry.
For additional information, please visit www.glww.org,
email info@glww.org, or write to Gospel Light Worldwide,
1957 Eastman Avenue, Ventura, CA 93003, U.S.A.

I dedicate this resource to the people who were an example of devotional living for me: my mom, my dad, my sisters and all the camp counselors I had a chance to grow up watching at Green Wing Bible Camp in Amboy, Illinois. Through all of you, God showed me that devotions were a way of life and not simply something you try to accomplish once a week.

# Contents

# Introduction

Welcome to the @ Home series of resources!

This series of booklets has been created for one simple reason: to help you bring true, life-enhancing Christian faith into the fabric of your everyday life at home.

If you are at all like the thousands of parents I have worked with over the past 16 years, you have a strong and even desperate desire to establish a more stable and healthy household than the one you grew up in. I believe parents today want to be good—if not great—parents and they want their children to grow up in a supportive and nurturing home environment. Parents today are open to bringing more of God into their lifestyle at home because they know that God can help them; they simply don't know how to make it work because it wasn't a part of the home environment they grew up in. Does this sound familiar to you?

I do not believe the problem many families face today is that they are led by bad or ungodly parents; it is that parents are unprepared because Satan has been at work to take Christ and Christ-like living out of the home. Let me be very clear: God wants what is best for you and your family. He wants you and your family to "enjoy long life" (Deuteronomy 6:2), and He has made provision for it. Yet His adversary, the devil, "prowls around like a roaring lion looking for someone to devour" (1 Peter 5:8). And the battleground is your home.

Satan doesn't want you living out your faith in your home. He doesn't want you praying, reading the Bible or engaging in faith-talk, devotions or worship in the home, because he doesn't want what is best for you and your family. His plot is to get you to believe that faith is something you outsource to the "experts" or express only when you are at church. This is a lie coming from "the father of lies" (John 8:44).

Unfortunately, this thinking creates a hypocritical reality where Christianity is something we do at church but not at home. Many young adults are walking away from the faith in alarming numbers because they grew up in this hypocritical environment. They are saying, "If that's what Christianity is, then I don't want anything to do with it."

A recent *New York Times* article reported that evangelical Christian leaders are warning one another that their teenagers are abandoning the faith in droves in spite of packed mega-churches. At an unusual series of leadership meetings in 44 cities this fall, more than 6,000 pastors heard dire forecasts from some of the biggest names in the conservative evangelical movement. Their alarm has been stoked by a claim that if current trends continue, only 4 percent of teenagers will be "Bible-believing Christians" as adults. That would be a sharp decline compared with 35 percent of the current generation of baby boomers, and before that, 65 percent of the World War II generation.[1]

The good news is that we serve a God of second chances. The God of the universe is again offering us the same basic faith skills that will help you, your children and your children's children enjoy long (eternal) life (see Deuteronomy 6:2).

Do you want to enjoy long, eternal life?

Do you want this for your children and your children's children?

Start looking at how you can bring faith back into the very center of your home!

This @ Home booklet will help you and your family establish one specific faith skill with multiple practical applications that you can incorporate into your "at home" lifestyle. The content of this booklet assumes that you have no idea how to do this faith skill at home because research indicates that even Christian households are not actively engaged in these basic faith practices. You will read some very compelling and inspirational stories of people who have had their lives transformed as a result of making this faith skill a part of their 24/7 lifestyle at home. And finally, you will find many practical ideas for all ages that will allow you to establish and maintain this faith skill in your home throughout the years.

May the Lord bless you as you establish your home as the primary place where faith is nurtured.

**Note**

1. Laurie Goodstein, "Evangelicals Fear the Loss of Their Teenagers," *New York Times*, October 6, 2006. http://www.ny
   times.com/2006/10/06/us/06evangelical.html.

# Attitude Check

I grew up as the son of a Bible camp director. My backyard was 500 acres with soccer and softball fields, horses, and lots of hiking trails. What made things even better was that for 10 weeks in the summer I would have 100 new friends to play with every week. Through the years I learned a lot of "camp tricks" that counselors used to keep the campers under control. One of those was an attitude check. Inevitably during each new week of camp, a series of episodes would occur that would cause the campers to be in a bad mood. It could be a rainstorm, mosquitoes or bad food. One of the tricks the counselors would use to get the campers out of their bad mood was to yell out, "Attitude Check!" When the campers heard this, they responded by yelling back, "Praise the Lord!" One time was never enough and the counselors would repeat the call again, yelling, "Attitude Check!" and the campers would loudly respond, "Praise the Lord!" And then the call would come one last time with even more vigor, "Attitude Check?" And all the campers would boldly respond,

"Praise the Lord!" In almost every situation the mood
had been instantly changed.

## Attitudes About Devotions

Sometimes we need an attitude check in our homes.
What is your attitude about doing family devotions
in your home? When you think about doing family
devotions, maybe you feel at a complete loss about
what to do. Maybe it produces images of trying to
corral your entire family for one or two hours where
you sit at the kitchen table with a candle burning,
reading the Bible together and singing "Kum Ba
Yah." The idea of family devotions terrifies people
for many reasons, because the idea of getting together, reading the Bible or singing together is not
something many have experienced. You know that
no one wants to do it, yet you cling to a small mea-
sure of hope that family devotions could actually
bring you closer together as a family.

To be perfectly honest, this is by far the most
difficult booklet in this series I have written. When
we were in discussion at Gospel Light about which
booklet should be done first, the devotions project
was near the top. I tried floating other ideas, but we
kept coming back to family devotions. I even tried
finding someone else to write this booklet. Finally,
with the deadline approaching, I had no choice but
to sit down and begin writing. My wife shared
something that served as the final push I needed:

"Maybe God wants you to write this booklet so we can get better at doing family devotions ourselves."

Understand that this material is not coming from an expert. I, too, struggle to find ways to engage in family devotions in our home with our 13-year-old daughter. I grew up in a Christian household but I don't remember ever having a formal, regular time of family devotions other than at Christmas time before we would open our Christmas presents. While my dad, as you will see in chapter 4, would lead devotions and Bible studies at camp where he served as a camp director, we didn't have a regular practice of having devotions together as a family at home.

I just don't have a lot of experience with leading devotions at home, at least not in the typical sense, and maybe that is why God has called me to write this booklet. I am on this journey too, with an authentic desire to grow closer as a family to God through family devotions. Yet, I also have to examine my attitude toward devotions, because I think they can be so much more than an arduous ritual. Do your own attitude check on this topic, and consider a new thing God may want to do in your family. Be open as you read to consider some new ways of having consistent devotional time with your children. Be open to consider a new attitude toward family devotions.

If your children are older, talk with them about their concepts about family devotions, whether you have them or not. Go through some of these questions together after thinking them through yourself.

**@Home Questions**

- What is your attitude toward doing family devotions? What would you like it to be?
- Did you ever experience family devotions growing up? Describe that experience.
- What is your picture of what family devotions are?

## A Challenge of Attitude

I'll never forget the attitude I had toward church when I was a teenager. It wasn't pretty. To sum it up, I hated going to church. As a teenager, I was given permission to move my bedroom into the unfinished basement of our home. Even though it had a concrete floor and was always cold and musty smelling, I thought it was heavenly because it was my space. I had my own living room, 8-track AM/FM stereo, and 15-inch black-and-white television that only got four channels using the rabbit ears. The icing on the cake was my king-sized, free flotation waterbed! When I got underneath the covers, that warm waterbed and dark basement made for the perfect sleeping environment.

Sunday mornings, usually after a late night with my friends, were not made for getting up early to go to church. They were a perfect time to sleep in. Yet every Sunday morning, without question, I would hear my mom yell down from the top of the base-ment steps, "Mark, time to get up and go to church." I would try to ignore it, but she would persist. And almost every Sunday morning I would respond, "Oh, Mom . . . do I have to go to church?" But there was never a response. She just left the lights on, which was an answer in itself.

I'll never forget the Sunday that everything changed. I was in my warm waterbed when out of the cold dark air came the cry, "Mark, time to get up and go to church." I responded as always, "Oh, Mom, do I have to go to church?" Only this time something changed. My mom responded, "No, Mark, you don't have to go to church." I couldn't believe it! I perked up and made her repeat it just to make sure I had heard what she said. "You don't have to go to church," she repeated, and I began thinking to myself, *There is a God after all!* I didn't have to go to church. I didn't have to get out of my warm waterbed and make the long trek across the cold basement floor and up the stairs to begin the process of getting ready for church. I didn't have to . . . I didn't have to . . . I didn't have to go to church! And then my mom made a fi-nal statement. "That's right, Mark, you don't have to go to church, you *get to* go to church." And with those words I was had! No response could be given. No comeback would work. With those words, my per-spective and attitude had been challenged and changed. "You don't have to go to church, *you get to go to church.*"

Maybe your journey toward family devotions needs to begin with this same type of attitude and perspective change. "You don't have to do devotions, *you get to do* devotions." The book of 1 Chronicles describes a situation in which King David instructs the people of Israel to help his son Solomon build a temple where they can honor, worship and glorify God: "David ordered all the leaders of Israel to help his son Solomon. He said to them, 'Is not the LORD your God with you? And has he not granted you rest on every side? For he has handed the inhabitants of the land over to me, and the land is subject to the LORD and to his people. Now devote your heart and soul to seeking the LORD your God'" (22:17-19). I love how David motivated them to be devoted; he reminded them of who God is and what God had done for them.

If your children are older and you have never had devotions as a family, you may find that their attitude is that they "have to" have these times rather than "they get to." Encourage them go through an adjustment process. Maybe a starting point for your family devotions is to remember who God is and what He has done for you. Devotions are not about what you do, but about what God has done and is doing all around you. It is something you get to do with those you love most so that you all can be closer to the God of the universe.

Would you like to know God better? Would you like to know God's plan and purposes for your life?

Would you like to be able to hear God's voice better? God knows, sees and understands things that you can't know, see or understand on your own. Wouldn't you like to get to know Him better? You have been given an opportunity to do that. God has handed this world over to those He created, a world that is big, confusing, overwhelming, complicated and intimidating; yet you have access to the Creator of this world. God is the engineer, designer, builder and chief architect. You can know His perspective and understanding. That's worth your time and devotion. In addition, God has a plan and purpose for your life that you can know better as you spend more time with Him.

Recently, I was hospitalized with a back injury. I would like to say that there was a specific cause, but there wasn't. It was a condition that steadily got worse because I refused to acknowledge a problem, and I kept doing all the things I was doing wrong without doing anything to take care of my back. My dad had a severe back condition that I had been told I was preconditioned to have as well. Through the years I had occasional problems with my back, but did I do anything about it? Nope. I began running two to four miles a day, four days a week, which started to bother my back, but did I stop? Nope. Then on a Monday, I played in a golf tournament, even though I woke up with a sore back that morning. My back continued to get worse and I played horribly, but did I stop? Of course not. That night I tossed and turned in pain, but did I take anything for it? Nope.

The next morning, I got on a plane for a four-hour flight to Chicago, which was to be the beginning of a 28-day speaking trip that would take me to four countries. My back continued to worsen, and I had another sleepless night. The next morning I could barely walk, and I had to speak at a conference to more than 1,500 youth pastors. Now I was desperate, so I called the leadership team of the conference and they got me to a doctor who pretty much said, "I can't do much for you now." Filled with pain medication, I made it through my keynote message; but just four hours later, I was in the emergency room, which ended up turning into an overnight stay so that a series of tests could be run.

The outcome of the tests was that I had three bulging discs. But did I stop the speaking tour? Nope. Thanks to a lot of prayer and medication, I was able to shuffle, toss and turn my way through the next 28 days. When I got home, my doctor got me into a physical therapist who told me, "Mark, you have a back that could get better or worse. You are teetering on the edge, and what you do next will decide which way this goes. You can have a life of back problems or you can choose to learn how to start taking care of your back. It's your decision." Let's just say that God got my attention, and for the first time in my life I was on a journey to learn and do whatever I needed to take care of my back. I now exercise differently and stretch continually in ways I never thought I would or could do.

In many ways, devotions are like this. You get to a teetering point in your relationship with and understanding of God. Your relationship with God can either get better or worse. You decide. Are you going to do some of the things you need to do so you can know and understand God and His ways better? I must confess that I am really enjoying some of the new exercises I'm learning to do. And for the first time my back is actually getting healthier. Friends, that is what will happen with having devotions. You will find yourself enjoying the new things you learn, and your overall relationship with God will get healthier. As you include your children in your time of devotions, they will have opportunities to grow closer to God, too.

I don't know how God got your attention or how this booklet ended up in your hands, but maybe it is time for you to look at what you need to do to become a healthier Christian. There are a lot of people who say they believe in God yet don't know what it's like to live a healthy Christ-following lifestyle. Is that you? Instead of doing something about it you just keep going through life doing one unhealthy thing after another, and your condition worsens. Would you like to get off that treadmill? Are you ready to explore some new things you can do that will help you become a healthy Christian? This isn't something you have to do. It's something you get to do!

## @Home Questions

- How have you learned about God and His ways in the past?
- What spiritual exercises do you currently do to become a healthier Christian?
- How much time do you spend a day doing spiritual exercises?
- How would you assess your current spiritual fitness level?
- What will increasing your spiritual health do for your children? What changes might you see in your family?

# 2

# Family Devotion Myths

When I travel and speak internationally, I often work with a translator. At first, this was uncomfortable and unsettling because I had to shorten my message—never easy for a pastor—and speak only one or two sentences at a time. It always takes awhile to get into a rhythm with your translator, and inevitably you run into a situation where the translator does not know how to translate an English word or phrase that you have used. This frequently happens when I use the word "devotions." I will quote the Barna Group statistic that reveals that less than 10 percent of Christian households pray, read the Bible or engage in any form of family devotions or worship in the home. The translator will begin translating the quote, but stops at the word "devotions" and asks me, "What do you mean when you say devotions?"

Even in our language, the word may have different meanings. What do you think of when you hear the word "devotions"? To best describe it, we'll start by dispelling some common myths regarding family devotions. This will lead us to a definition of family devotions that may be quite different from any other definition you have previously encountered or experienced.

## Myth #1
### Family Devotions Are
### Long and Boring

Could this be true? Yes, but it doesn't have to be that way. Some people have the notion that family devotions require the family to sit together quietly for at least an hour at the kitchen table reading the Bible with a candle burning. I am not trying to offend anyone who has had this form of family devotions, and I am not saying this cannot work in some situations. The point is that it is a myth to believe this is the only way your family can engage in family devotions.

We live in a great time where there are all sorts of fun and creative ways to engage in family devotions. Family devotions can take place in the minivan, on vacation, in the bedroom, while taking a bike ride or while having a Happy Meal at McDonalds. You can use a computer, DVD player, the Internet, books and magazines to engage in family devotions. And some of the best family devotions you will have will happen in five minutes or less. Many times family devotions will simply be a short conversation about an experience you just had as a family where you discuss together how God was at work in and through that situation. Your family devotions may take place on the 10-minute ride home from school or at your child's bedside before he or she goes to sleep each evening. No matter what age your children are, short conversations and messages from parents are usually more effective than longer discussions. Family devotions can take many different styles and forms.

# Myth #2

## We Don't Have to Do Family Devotions Because Our Kids Are Involved at Church or Attend a Christian School

Do you believe the church is the primary place where faith is nurtured? I truly believe that is one of Satan's biggest lies and greatest strategies to take down Christianity. Don't fall for it. Don't buy into it. Don't be deceived. The home is the primary place where faith is nurtured. The Bible depicts this in Deuteronomy 6:4-9:

> Hear, O Israel: The LORD our God, the LORD is one. Love the LORD your God with all your heart and with all your soul and with all your strength. These commandments that I give you today are to be upon your hearts. Impress them on your children. Talk

about them when you sit *at home* and when you walk along the road, *when you lie down and when you get up*. Tie them as symbols on your hands and bind them on your foreheads. Write them on the doorframes of your *houses and on your gates* (emphasis added).

Did you see where you are to engage in faith-talk and devotions? Three of the four references depict it as happening in your home. I could also show you one research study after another that would confirm this. You need to know that what mom and dad do at home is two to three times more influential than any church program when it comes to influencing kids toward faithful living. The church has some great things to offer you and your family that you should definitely take advantage of. Yet you have to understand that what happens at church is meant to enhance—not replace—what happens in your home. So let me be crystal clear: Family devotions are more influential in shaping the long-term faith walk of your children than any church program you sign them up for, no matter how good the program is.

Do you want your kids to have a lasting faith? Do you want them to have the type of faith that will stick with them forever? The type of faith that will influence the myriad life decisions that they will make? Then you have to set the example of living a wholly devoted life through the devotional way you live your life at home. From the time your children enter your home until they leave to make their own home, what you do and say and who you are as a believer in Christ is impacting their lives for eternity.

## Myth #3:

### You Have to Have All the Answers to Lead Family Devotions

The number-one reason why most parents probably do not engage in leading family devotions is the fear that their children will ask a question they don't know how to answer. Well, let me handle this as gently as I can. Get over it and get used to it. I'm a pastor who has had years of seminary training, and my daughter asks me questions all the time that I can't answer. In fact, those are some of our best devotional times when we have to wrestle with something we don't understand about God or how He works, or something the Bible says. Your role as a parent in family devotions is not so much about giving answers as it is about creating an environment where anyone can ask and together you can wrestle with the questions of life. That is where true faith comes to the forefront. All you can do is share what you have been given for ideas, insights or experiences, and look into God's Word for what He has already shared there.

One of my favorite passages of Scripture is found in Luke 2:46-50 where Jesus, who was almost

a teenager at the time, left his parents and was
found in the temple, sitting with a lot of educated
adults, discussing faith and life with them. This is a
perfect example of what a time of devotions should
look like:

> After three days they found him in the tem-
> ple courts, sitting among the teachers, lis-
> tening to them and asking them questions.
> Everyone who heard him was amazed at his
> understanding and his answers. When his
> parents saw him, they were astonished. His
> mother said to him, "Son, why have you
> treated us like this? Your father and I have
> been anxiously searching for you." "Why
> were you searching for me?" he asked.
> "Didn't you know I had to be in my Father's
> house?" But they did not understand what
> he was saying to them.

I notice three things in this passage. First, Jesus is
"listening to [the teachers] and asking them questions" (v. 50). Jesus is asking questions and not just
providing answers! Devotions are meant to be a time
when you openly ask questions because you come to
understand where each other is coming from through
the questions you ask. Jesus gained a better understanding of where people were coming from. Jesus
wanted to connect with them where they were, and He
used questions to dial into their life situations.

I recently came home from a lunch meeting to find that my wife was in the middle of a time of weekly Bible study she leads with our daughter and her two best friends. I knew better than to interrupt, so I stayed in our downstairs living room while they met in our upstairs kitchen and dining room area. I found myself drawn into their discussion as I listened to them ask each other how they would handle themselves as Christians in different life situations. Each one would ask a question or present a scenario and all the others would answer how they would handle themselves in that situation. The questions drove the discussion, and each person contributed questions as well as answers. That is the same type of environment Jesus created when He was in the temple courts—an environment where everyone, including Jesus, was asking questions.

The second thing I notice in the Luke passage is that "everyone who heard him was amazed at his understanding and his answers" (v. 47). Be prepared to be amazed at the way God will answer your questions. God doesn't shy away from questions. He wants to answer them. So be prepared to get answers when you turn to Him and His Word with your questions.

And finally, when Jesus talked, "they did not understand what he was saying to them" (v. 50). Unfortunately, you may not always understand the answers God gives, and that's just a fact you are going to have to live with. Even those who knew

Jesus best, His earthly parents and His disciples, did not understand Him all the time. Neither will you. It is something you need to be prepared to admit to one another.

So what can be learned from this example of Jesus? Devotions are a time for asking questions, receiving some answers from the Lord and expecting that there will be things you don't understand.

## Myth #4:
### Family Devotions Require Hours of Preparation

Nowhere in the Bible will you find a passage that tells you must prepare for many hours before engaging in faith-talk or family devotions. Engaging in family devotions is not like preparing to give a lesson plan or keynote presentation. Leading effective family devotions does not require you to have all your ducks in a row, complete with a theme, four Scripture passages and multiple teaching points, each with a different illustration. Don't get caught up in continually looking for a curriculum, DVD or book to help you lead family devotions. Don't wait until you have all the crayons, glue sticks and cardboard cutouts ready to go before even starting. It is helpful to have some sort of plan for engaging your family in devotions on a regular basis. Yet you need to be careful not to over-program or over-prepare for family devotions. Be prepared and ready to engage in family devotions anytime and anywhere because God is at work at all times and in all situations. Could you lead family devotions without a curriculum or lesson plan? Absolutely!

As a Bible camp director, one of the things my dad taught all of his camp counselors to do was to continually look for teachable moments. Teachable moments are simply opportunities to engage in faith conversations while doing ordinary things that transpire during a day. Dad simply said, "Be prepared at any time to bring God into the conversation or situation." We could be on a walk and someone would see a snake; this would open the door as a teachable moment to ask a simple question like, "Why do you think Satan is depicted as a snake?" Or seeing a bullfrog would prompt the question, "Why do you think God created bullfrogs?" It was amazing to hear all the answers from one simple question and teachable moment.

Having devotions through teachable moments is something I use with my daughter. Recently, we drove by a homeless person who was holding a sign asking for money, and we didn't stop and give him anything. Instead of saying nothing, I asked our daughter what she thought of the fact that we didn't stop and give the homeless person any money. That led to a 15-minute teachable moment where we wrestled with a myriad questions regarding how Christians should respond to the plight of the homeless. Was I prepared for a devotion on this topic?

Not in the least. But a teachable moment raised some great discussion and questions that we continue to wrestle through.

## Myth #5:

### You Have to Be a Biblical Scholar or Expert to Lead Family Devotions

We live in a time when just about everything is outsourced to the "experts." If you don't feel like fixing a chicken dinner, let the experts do it at your favorite restaurant. If you don't know how to get a stain out of a shirt, take it to the experts at the drycleaners. If you don't have the time or an interest in maintaining your housework, hire housecleaners. And when it comes to raising your kids spiritually, just drop them off at church or enroll them in Sunday School, youth ministry or Christian school where the "experts" can teach them all they need to know about faith.

Nowhere in the Bible will you find a verse that says, "Pass your faith on to your children by taking them to church and letting the experts do it for you." Instead, Deuteronomy 6:7 says, "Impress them [the ways of God] on your children. Talk about them when you sit at home and when you walk along the road, when you lie down and when you get up." God has given you what you need to lead family devotions. Trust Him. You also have two things going for you: First, chances are that no one in your household has ever participated in family devotions before, so they won't know if you're doing it right or wrong; second, there is no right or wrong way to have family devotions. It is the ultimate win/win situation! You can't go wrong because there is no expectation or standard that you must meet.

Martin Luther once wrote that parents are called to be the "bishops, apostles and priests of their own homes."[1] So there you have it. You are now a pastor, or better yet, bishop, of your own home. Go and lead devotions, trusting that God will guide and lead you.

## Myth #6:
### You Have to Stop Everything Else You Are Doing to Do Family Devotions

Have you ever tried to get your entire family all together, at one time, doing the same thing? Next to parting the Red Sea, accomplishing this for most families might be one of the greatest miracles of God. While it may be considered the best-case scenario for you to stop everything else you are doing to have family devotions, I would like to challenge this line of thinking. As a camp director's kid, I witnessed many campers have great encounters and experiences with God at Bible camp. What is it about Bible camp that makes it so effective at leading people closer to God? I would argue that Bible camp is effective because God and faith-talk at camp is woven into everything you do. You don't stop and do devotions at camp. You live a devoted, 24/7 Christian lifestyle at camp where everything you do has a Christian purpose to it. Imagine if family devotions became less of something you had to do and more of a way you live!

Embed your devotions throughout your day. Sing songs about Jesus to your babies as you change their diapers. Squat down with your toddlers and observe how the ants in the yard each have a job as helpers to get things done, just like the family of God. Develop a "family of God hug" with your preschoolers squished in the middle that any family member can call for any time of the day. Talk out loud to God conversationally around your young children as you go through the day so they can see what your relationship with God is like. Reminisce at night with your older children about how God was with them and took care of them in each of their activities throughout the day. Talk with your teens about current news items you see on TV and how people make choices based on what flows out of their hearts. Make devotions part of your life, not something disconnected from what you are already doing.

## Devotions Defined

This review of myths leads to a definition for family devotions: Family devotions are simply the way you bring Christ and Christ-like living into your daily lives as individuals and as a family. Devotions are about seeking God at all times, in all you do. Devotions are about living a wholly devoted life to God that is continually seeking, wrestling with and applying the truths of God's Word to your daily walk. The question is not, "Are you ready to do family devotions?" The question is, "Are you ready, as a family, to be devotional at all times and in all places?" With that as your target, you are ready to further explore how to make family devotions a way of life rather than something you have to do once a week.

**Note**

1. Martin Luther, "The Estate of Marriage, 1522" in Walther Brand, ed., *Luther's Works* (Philadelphia: Fortress Press, 1962), p. 46.

# 3

# Devotional Tools

As a pastor, speaker and author, I have the gift of gab, meaning that I am quite comfortable speaking in front of people. Unfortunately, there are a lot of gifts I do not have, including the ability to work on cars or house projects. Recently, we decided to put a new wood laminate floor in our kitchen, and to my wife's amazement, I was able to do the job without any professional help. What was the key? I had a friend who did this all the time, and he gave me the right advice and the right tools to work with. He told me, "Mark, half the battle is having the right tools." My tool supply is not very extensive, but when I had his tools to work with, I found the job much easier to accomplish. In the same way, as we seek to become devotional families who have devotional moments at any time, half the battle is having the right tools. Here are some important tools to help you be devotional.

## Tool #1:
### A Personal Relationship with God

The first tool is found in Deuteronomy 6:4-6: "Hear, O Israel: The LORD our God, the LORD is one. Love the LORD your God with all your heart and with all your soul and with all your strength. These commandments that I give you today are to be upon your hearts."

Did you notice what must come first before you can impress anything on your children? It is you being in a loving relationship with God. Here are the critical questions: Are you in love with God? Are you living in such a way that your children and friends would say you are in love with God? Your children are going to be impressed and ultimately in love with whoever you are in love with. Devotional living starts with being in a devoted relationship with Jesus Christ. God sent Jesus here to earth, and in Him you have a human form of God to know, follow and love.

Your devotional life begins with your being in a devoted relationship with Jesus Christ. Your kids will be devoted to whoever and whatever you are devoted to. When you are in a devoted relationship with God, you will then look for Him and see Him 24/7. Teachable moments will surround you all the time because God is in all things. Yet if you are only partially devoted to God, then you will only partially see Him. That's why Deuteronomy 6:5 says, "Love the LORD your God with *all* your heart and with *all* your soul and with *all* your strength" (emphasis added). So what is the best thing you can do to increase your devotional life as a family? Increase your devotion to Jesus Christ.

And just in case you are wondering why you would want to do this—why you would want to live in a fully devoted life to Jesus Christ—remember Deuteronomy 6:2: "So that you, your children and their children after them may fear the LORD your God as long as you live by keeping all his decrees and commands that I give you, and so that you may enjoy long life." You live a fully devoted life to Christ "so that" you, your children and your grandchildren will enjoy long, eternal life together in heaven. Great reason!

## Tool #2:

### God's Word

The next tool you will need for devotions is God's Word. I love the Bible because it is God's living Word, and it speaks each time you open it. I've always wondered why the Bible isn't the most read book in households. Think about it. This is the God of the universe—who created the heavens and the earth and who knows all things—speaking directly to you. It is not an outdated history book. It is God's living Word that communicates His truth, advice and love to you. Do you read the Bible just for pleasure? Is it the first resource you turn to for advice and counsel? The Bible should be the most used tool in your tool belt.

For many people, the reason they don't turn to the Bible is simply that they don't know how to use this tool. Let me provide a few pieces of information that may help you use the Bible more effectively.

## A Concordance

You can purchase a concordance as a separate book or get a Bible with a concordance. What is a concordance? It is simply a reference guide, an index, which helps you navigate your way around the Bible. With a concordance you can look up key words, like "anger," "suffering," "joy," "peace," and so on, and find a list Scripture passages with those key words in them.

So let's say your daughter is facing temptations that are luring her away from God's way. You can go to you concordance and look up the word "temptation" and find these passages, among others:

- Matthew 26:41: "Watch and pray so that you will not fall into temptation. The spirit is willing, but the body is weak."

- Luke 22:39-40: "Jesus went out as usual to the Mount of Olives, and his disciples followed him. On reaching the place, he said to them, 'Pray that you will not fall into temptation.'"

- 1 Corinthians 10:12-13: "So, if you think you are standing firm, be careful that you don't fall! No temptation has seized you except what is common to man. And God is faithful; he will not let you be tempted beyond what you can bear. But when you are tempted, he will also provide a way out so that you can stand up under it."

· James 1:12-15: "Blessed is the man who perseveres under trial, because when he has stood the test, he will receive the crown of life that God has promised to those who love him. When tempted, no one should say, 'God is tempting me.' For God cannot be tempted by evil, nor does he tempt anyone; but each one is tempted when, by his own evil desire, he is dragged away and enticed. Then, after desire has conceived, it gives birth to sin; and sin, when it is full-grown, gives birth to death."

Do you see how easily you and your daughter can now have a devotional conversation about temptation? You don't need to have the Bible memorized. I need help finding biblical answers to life issues just like anyone else, and that's where a concordance helps out. With a concordance, you have access to God's Word and counsel for your life. You do not need to come up with answers on you own. You can let God's Word speak for itself.

### A Topical Bible
Another similar tool to a concordance is a topical Bible. The Bible I tend to use the most is a Youth Bible because it provides a great list of topics in the

front that I can go through and find biblical answers to. For example, some of the topics include peer pressure, church, death, discouragement, fear, giving, leadership, money, worrying and worship. When you look up a topic, the topical Bible guides you to five or six passages that provide a biblical insight or perspective on that topic. In most topical Bibles you also have a modern story or illustration that helps explain the biblical passage on the topic you are exploring.

One of the things my daughter and I do on occasion is simply open the Youth Bible and pick a topic. Sometimes I pick the topic and sometimes she does. Then we go through some of the passages that are provided to help us understand how God wants us to understand and respond to that topic. It's a very easy way to have devotions any time and anywhere without having to prepare in advance.

## Multiple Translations

Another tool is to have a couple different translations of the Bible. Sometimes you may not understand something in the Bible. That is okay. Some things in the Bible are difficult to understand; yet if you look at the passage in a different translation, you may have more understanding. For example, my wife reads one translation of the Bible, while I read another version, and my daughter reads a third. It is always fun to hear how each version translates a passage, and many times that is what leads us to a better understanding of the passage. I would recommend that every household have at least one standard translation of the Bible, such as *New International Version* or *New American Standard Bible*, along with a modern or contemporary version, like the *New Century Version* or *THE MESSAGE*. Here is a passage from James 1:12-15 on temptation in various translations.

- *New International Version (NIV)*: "Blessed is the man who perseveres under trial, because when he has stood the test, he will receive the crown of life that God has promised to those who love him. When tempted, no one should say, 'God is tempting me.' For God cannot be tempted by evil, nor does he tempt anyone; but each one is tempted when, by his own evil desire, he is dragged away and enticed. Then, after desire has conceived, it gives birth to sin; and sin, when it is full-grown, gives birth to death."

- *New American Standard Version (NASB)*: "Blessed is a man who perseveres under trial; for once he has been approved, he will receive the crown of life which the Lord has promised to those who love Him. Let no one say when he is tempted, 'I am being tempted by God'; for God cannot be tempted by evil, and He Himself does not tempt anyone. But each one is tempted when he is carried away and enticed by his own lust. Then when lust has conceived, it gives birth to sin; and when sin is accomplished, it brings forth death."

- *New Century Version (NCV):* "When people are tempted and still continue strong, they should be happy. After they have proved their faith, God will reward them with life forever. God promised this to all those who love him. When people are tempted, they should not say, 'God is tempting me.' Evil cannot tempt God, and God himself does not tempt anyone. But people are tempted when their own evil desire leads them away and traps them. This desire leads to sin, and then the sin grows and brings death."

- *THE MESSAGE:* "Anyone who meets a testing challenge head-on and manages to stick it out is mighty fortunate. For such persons loyally in love with God, the reward is life and more life. Don't let anyone under pressure to give in to evil say, 'God is trying to trip me up.' God is impervious to evil, and puts evil in no one's way. The temptation to give in to evil comes from

us and only us. We have no one to blame
but the leering, seducing flare-up of our
own lust. Lust gets pregnant, and has a
baby: sin! Sin grows up to adulthood, and
becomes a real killer."

If you have young children in your home, be
sure to get a children's Bible. There are different
kinds. Some are in a specific Bible version, like the
*New International Version*, but include illustrations
and sidebars with stories and topics that relate to
children. Some contain the main Bible stories with
illustrations. Make sure that each person in your
family has his or her own Bible, and get your young
children used to reading and looking at their
Bibles often.

## Digital Libraries

A final resource that I believe every household
should invest in is some form of digital library that
can be downloaded or installed on your computer.
Digital libraries, like Libronix, provide an easy way
for you to have a concordance, topical guides, multiple translations and commentaries that help explain passages all in one place. In a matter of minutes
you can navigate through the Bible using multiple
sources and tools found in your digital library.
Many times, kids, who are more technologically
savvy than parents, can use this tool in better ways
than you ever imagined possible.

The Bible is the greatest tool in our devotional tool belt, and you need to take advantage of it and related resources. As with anything, the more you use it the better you will get at using it. Remember, God wants to speak to you through His Word. God wants to be understood and He wants to speak into your life. Don't be intimidated by the Bible. Take advantage of the fact that we have tools like concordances, topical Bibles, multiple translations and digital libraries to help us connect with God through His Word.

# Tool #3:

## Music

Music is another tool you can use to communicate your feelings in your devotions. Music can settle you down and prepare you to spend time with God. It is amazing how music can speak to your heart. A certain song can say or reflect something you have been feeling.

One of the things my family likes to do when we are preparing to spend time talking about God together is to simply listen to a couple of Christian songs together. Sometimes we pick the song in advance because one of us has a song we have heard that we want to share, while other times we will just turn on the Christian radio station and listen to whatever is playing. In either case, the music usually speaks to our hearts and even gives us something to talk about regarding God. Ask your older children and teens to share with you some of their favorite music. Find out what the words are saying and why they like it. Learn to appreciate the differences in music preferences within your family. Help your children understand that different types of music help different people connect to God. Talk about the different styles of worship music you hear on the radio and in church and how it leads people closer to God.

## Tool #4:

### Online Messages

We live in a day when we have access to some of the greatest Bible preachers and teachers from all over the world. A simple way to engage in devotions is to listen to an online message from one of your favorite pastors. Many pastors and churches post their messages online for free, and all you have to do is pull it up on your computer or download it to your iPod and listen to it.

Recently, we have started having "home worship" where we listen to a couple of Christian songs followed by a message from one of our favorite pastors we like to listen to. Talk about an easy way to engage in devotions and faith-talk. We can pick the music and topic we like. It is like we are worship DJs! In saying this, let me be clear that I'm not saying this should replace going to church. You should still be connected to and engaged with a church where you worship together as a family with other believers. Taking advantage of online messages is simply a fun and easy way to have worship devotions at home.

# Tool #5:
## Your Eyes and Ears

I am writing this as I fly over the Rocky Mountains on my way from Denver back to Los Angeles. As I look out my window, I see one of the most awesome works of God—the snow-capped mountains that cascade to deep green flatlands with beautiful blue lakes. If my daughter were sitting next to me, this would be one of the easiest devotional times ever as we simply sat in awe of God's creation. Some of the greatest devotional tools at your disposal are your eyes and ears. How many times do you simply miss the works of God all around you?

When you slow down and take time to look for God and listen for His voice, it is truly amazing what you will see and hear. Now, I'm not saying you will see the face of God or hear His audible voice, but you will see and hear things that shape your view and understanding of who God is. When was the last time you sat outside on a clear evening and looked at the stars, or went on a hike through the woods and looked at all the vegetation and wildlife He created, or watched the busy bugs in your yard?

We recently took our niece to the zoo. It opened up some great devotional conversation.

A simple way to have devotions where you take advantage of your eyes and ears is to give everyone 10 to 20 minutes to go on a walk, looking and listening for God. Give everyone a pad of paper or digital camera and write down or take pictures of things you see and hear. If you have young children, have mom take one and dad take one (or more, if you have more than two) and do this activity with your kids. Come back together and share the things you heard and saw. Do this one time during the morning, another time in the afternoon, as well as in the evening. You will be amazed at all the ways God surrounds you throughout the day.

## Tool #6:

### Devotional Resources

Go to a Christian bookstore or perform an Internet search for "family devotions" and you will quickly see that there is a lot of great stuff out there. There is no lack of good material; we probably live in a time when there are more devotional resources than ever before. There are devotional resources for the home, car, workplace and school, as well as resources for children, teens, young adults, singles, moms, dads, single parents, grandparents and stepparents. There are devotional games, faith-talk cards, conversation starters and Bible trivia. Talk to other families you know and find out what resources they use. Borrow and loan resources among several families to keep things fresh. Make use of the endless resources you have access to that will help you engage in family devotions any time and all the time. Pick something and just get started.

# 4

# Devotions for Your Home

So far in this book, we have done an attitude check, uncovered myths about devotions and looked at some tools to help you be devotional at any time. In this last chapter are devotions you can use in your home. My dad, affectionately known at camp as Uncle Arlie, was one of the best I have ever seen at leading devotions any time and anywhere. For over 22 years as a camp director, he would train college-age staff to seize teachable moments and lead devotions in any situation. My dad would lead by example all summer by simply walking around camp having devotional moments with kids as they stood in line for breakfast, played soccer, were on a nature hike or sat by the campfire. Dad was truly incredible at creating a 24/7 devotional lifestyle at camp, and he impacted the lives of hundreds of camp counselors and thousands of children.

In the fall of 2002, my Dad was diagnosed with a terminal lung condition. We were told he would have about two years to live, and he passed away on

Thanksgiving eve of 2004. One of the hidden blessings we received was having two years to have a lot of great times and conversations together. In the summer of 2004, I preached a series on the Lord's Prayer. We wanted the messages to be family friendly, so one of the things we planned were family devotions to go with the sermon series. I instantly thought of my dad. I asked if he still had it in him to write a series of devotions on the Lord's Prayer we could give to the families of our congregation. Little did I know then that he would go to be with the Lord just five months later, making these the last devotions he would write.

Now, six years later, as I write a booklet on devotions for families, I find to my surprise that the first three chapters came together easily. As I considered what to do with the final chapter, I looked at my bookshelf and there, sitting by itself, was my one copy of "Holmen Family Devotionals" that my dad had written. I'd like to share them with you. In this chapter are six, easy-to-do anywhere, anytime devotionals as written by my dad, Uncle Arlie, whose passion was to help families have camp-like devotions at home. They have been modified some to help families with children of different ages. As you go through them, you will adapt them for your family as well.

Begin these devotions by having someone read the focus from the Lord's Prayer and the Scripture passage that has been selected. The Scripture passage is from the *New Century Version* of the Bible because this version is easier for children to understand. If your children are very young, read only a short portion of the passage or retell the stories from the Bible passage in your own words. Some stories would work well to act them out.

After someone has read the Scripture passage, read through "Uncle Arlie's Story" as a family. I would encourage you, as parents, to first read the story to see if you have a similar story or example to share from your life that would connect to the purpose and passage of the devotion. Your story will mean more to your children.

After the story has been read or shared, go through some of the discussion questions together. These questions are just a guide. You may not want to use all the questions or you may come up with questions that better apply to your family. The first questions are good for even young children. The questions become increasingly challenging, requiring some thought and application, which is especially good for older children and teenagers. You may want to let your children ask questions on the topic for other family members to answer.

When you have completed your discussion, close your devotional time in prayer as a family.

The basic format is the same for each devotional, and you can use it to develop your own devotions as well:

- Theme/topic
- Bible passage (which you can find using your concordance)
- Personal story
- Discussion questions
- Prayer

## Family Devotion #1

### Devotional Focus
"Our Father in heaven, may your name always be kept holy" (Matthew 6:9, *NCV*).

### Scripture Reading
"When you pray, don't be like those people who don't know God. They continue saying things that mean nothing, thinking that God will hear them because of their many words. Don't be like them, because your Father knows the things you need before you ask him" (Matthew 6:7-8, *NCV*).

### Purpose
To help you better understand your relationship to God as Father in your role as parents, son and daughter. To know that God is not some faraway God but a Father who is in your presence daily, if you let Him.

### Uncle Arlie's Story
I grew up on a farm in southern Minnesota, and attended grade school during World War II. I remem-

ber when my father was called up for the draft to become a soldier. My two younger brothers were not old enough to understand how this would affect us as a family. My mother and I wondered how we could ever manage the farm without him. I was only in third grade and could help milk the cows and feed the pigs and chickens, but I was not old enough to run the machinery, nor could my mother.

We were relieved when we got word that my dad was given a deferment because of his young family and the farm crops that would be needed to help feed all Americans, especially our soldiers. It was many years before I realized just how much I needed to have a father and mother who provided for us as a family during difficult times. I know that God, my heavenly Father, was looking out for us too.

I am grateful for parents who led me to become a child of God and who brought me to church and Sunday School every week. My pastor and teachers helped me know that God is my Father and that He cares very much about what goes on in my life. Whether my own father had been in my home or not, my heavenly Father would have continued to take care of me. Jesus called God, "Abba," which in the Hebrew language means "Daddy." Jesus talked to Him every day to stay connected and know what He should do. I talk to Him every day, too, because I want to be close to God my Father.

Sometimes you might think it's hard to talk to God or that you have to say just the right thing, but

Jesus knows what you need before you say it. Don't be afraid to say whatever is on your heart. God wants you to call upon Him with your worship, prayer, praise and thanksgiving. Keep God's name holy and be careful not to use it in an unholy way. It's a busy world, but you need to take time to talk to God, your Father. He's your "Daddy," and he loves you and wants to help you in your daily life. It is also a good idea for families to get together and include Father God in your family.

Discussion

1. What is a good father like? How is God like a good father?
2. How have your parents helped you to know your heavenly Father better? Who else has had a part in your spiritual growth?
3. How do you know that God is your Father who cares very much about what goes on in your life?
4. How easy is it for you to talk to your heavenly Father every day? When do you talk to Him? What is your conversation like?
5. If God already knows what you need, why do you think you need to ask Him?
6. When are some times we already talk to God together as a family? When else can we pray together? Are we ready to make a commitment to do this? What can we do to help us remember our decision to pray together?

Family Prayer Time

Close with a "popcorn" prayer where everyone completes the sentence, "Thank You God for being a 'daddy' who . . ." Keep sharing answers until everyone's prayers have been popped.

# Family Devotion #2

Devotional Focus

"May your kingdom come and what you want be done, here on earth as it is in heaven" (Matthew 6:10, *NCV*).

Scripture Reading

"Jesus went with his followers to a place called Gethsemane. He said to them, 'Sit here while I go over there and pray.' He took Peter and the two sons of Zebedee with him, and he began to be very sad and troubled. He said to them, 'My heart is full of sorrow, to the point of death. Stay here and watch with me.'

"After walking a little farther away from them, Jesus fell to the ground and prayed, 'My Father, if it is possible, do not give me this cup of suffering. But do what you want, not what I want.'

"Then Jesus went back to his followers and found them asleep. He said to Peter, 'You men could not stay awake with me for one hour? Stay awake and pray for strength against temptation. The spirit wants to do what is right, but the body is weak.'

"Then Jesus went away a second time and

prayed, 'My Father, if it is not possible for this painful thing to be taken from me, and if I must do it, I pray that what you want will be done'" (Matthew 26:36-42, *NCV*).

## Purpose
To help you as a family and individually know that the kingdom of God is within you—mom, dad, son, daughter, sister, brother and friend. You are a part of His kingdom when you live according to His will, not yours.

## Uncle Arlie's Story
Growing up in Minnesota winter meant one thing: snow! And lots of it. When the snowplows plowed the streets around our school, there were snow banks as high as California mountains. At least that's what it seemed like to me as a grade-schooler who had never seen Californian mountains. And it meant only one thing. Recess! And playing king of the mountain. I remember climbing on top of a snow bank and challenging anyone to throw me off. This was *my* kingdom! Sometimes I'd stay up there the whole recess, and sometimes my kingdom was taken away, especially when I became too confident.

In Matthew 4:8-11, you can read about the time when Satan tempted Jesus by showing Jesus all the kingdoms of the world. Satan offered to give all those kingdoms to Jesus if only Jesus would fall down and worship him. What was Jesus' reply to

Satan? (You'll have to look it up to find out for yourselves.)

I have often learned the hard way that when I become too proud or overconfident and want to do things my way instead of seeking what God's will is for me, that is when I usually get into trouble. Did you ever get in trouble for doing things your way instead of what your parents told you to do? (Parents, you need to answer this question as well.) The kingdom of God is not orbiting the earth like the moon (a good way to explain orbiting is to stand in the center of the room and have your child circle around you). The kingdom of God is within you when you first seek God's will for your life. You can know the happiness and joy of God's kingdom today if you just live according to His will. You have to choose: Your way or God's way.

## Discussion

1. Think of a time when you and someone else had two different ways for doing something, and one of you put aside your way for the other person's plan. How is this like doing things God's way rather than your own?

2. Describe a time you when you wanted something your way, not God's. What happened? What did you learn from that experience?

3. What might have happened if Jesus had done what He wanted instead of what God wanted when He was faced with death?

4. How do you know what God's will is?
5. What things in your life are you praying for His will to be done and not yours?
6. Martin Luther said we are to be "little Christs" and in this way help accomplish His will on earth as it is in heaven. Go around and let each family member complete the sentence, "I have seen God's will being done on earth through you when . . ."

Family Prayer Time
Alphabet Prayer: As a family, join hands praying in alphabetical order by first names. Or pray in reverse alphabetical order. Continue to pray until each person has had a chance to pray aloud.

# Family Devotion #3

Devotional Focus
"Give us the food we need for each day" (Matthew 6:11, NCV).

Scripture Reading
"Ask, and God will give to you. Search, and you will find. Knock, and the door will open for you. Yes, everyone who asks will receive. Everyone who searches will find. And everyone who knocks will have the door opened.

"If your children ask for bread, which of you would give them a stone? Or if your children ask for a fish, would you give them a snake? Even though you are bad, you know how to give good gifts to your children. How much more your heavenly Father will give good things to those who ask him!" (Matthew 7:7-11, *NCV*).

## Purpose

Think about how to move from a "gimmee" relationship with God to a relationship where you are content and happy for what God has given you, and to trust God to meet your needs.

## Uncle Arlie's Story

After serving in three different congregations, I accepted a call to become the executive director of a Bible camp. People of all ages, places and races came to camp. One of our largest ministries was in one of the nation's most dangerous neighborhoods where gunshots were heard daily. Yet right in the middle of 40-story apartment buildings sat a little red brick church. Poverty was everywhere; and even though the church was riddled with bullets, and the windows were covered with iron bars; the church served children one healthy meal a day. For many children this was the only good meal they would receive that day. In addition, most children wore clothes that had been passed down many times.

I would drive the white camp bus right into the middle of this area. I could hardly get off the bus before it was surrounded with kids jumping up and down saying, "Uncle Arlie's here!" What always amazed me was the amount of joy and happiness these kids had. It did not matter to them that they didn't have nice clothes, shoes or even decent meals. We would bring these kids to a week of camp. They were the kids that were the last to complain. They loved and cherished everything, from the meals we served (which to be perfectly honest were not always that good—it was camp food) to the squeaky bunk beds they had to sleep in, to the outhouses they had to use. What an example of gratefulness for God's provision!

Discussion

1. Do you have the idea that if you could just have more stuff you would be satisfied and happy? List 10 things you are grateful to God for providing. Can you name 20? How about 30?

2. What are some of the things you have asked God for? How has God responded?

3. What are you asking God for at this time? What does this prayer mean: "Give us the food we need for each day." In what ways has God given you what you need each day?

4. Do you find yourself complaining that you don't have enough when in reality you have more than enough? Gimmee, gimmee, gimmee—I promise I will never ask for anything else! Is God like a gumball machine? Put a quarter in, turn the knob and out pops just what you wanted? What are some ways you can put a stop to the pattern of

asking selfishly? What do you think God wants you to ask for?

### Family Prayer Time

Give everyone a pad of paper and pen and take five minutes to walk around and write down things to give God thanks for. Let young children dictate to you or let them draw pictures of what they see. Set a time for five minutes, and when the time is up have everyone come back together and share a prayer of thanks for the things on your lists.

## Family Devotion #4

### Devotional Focus

"Forgive us for our sins, just as we have forgiven those who sinned against us" (Matthew 6:12, *NCV*).

### Scripture Reading

"Peter came to Jesus and asked, 'Lord, when my fellow believer sins against me, how many times must I forgive him? Should I forgive him as many as seven times?'

Jesus answered, 'I tell you, you must forgive him more than seven times. You must forgive him even if he does wrong to you seventy times seven.

'The kingdom of heaven is like a king who decided to collect the money his servants owed him. When the king began to collect his money, a servant who owed him several million dollars was brought to him. But the servant did not have enough money to pay his master, the king. So the master ordered that every-thing the servant owned should be sold, even the servant's wife and children. Then the money would be used to pay the king what the servant owed.

'But the servant fell on his knees and begged, "Be patient with me, and I will pay you everything I owe." The master felt sorry for his servant and told him he did not have to pay it back. Then he let the servant go free.

'Later, that same servant found another servant who owed him a few dollars. The servant grabbed him around the neck and said, "Pay me the money you owe me!"

'The other servant fell on his knees and begged him, "Be patient with me, and I will pay you every-thing I owe."

'But the first servant refused to be patient. He threw the other servant into prison until he could pay everything he owed. When the other servants saw what had happened, they were very sorry. So they went and told their master all that had happened.

'Then the master called his servant in and said, "You evil servant! Because you begged me to forget what you owed, I told you that you did not have to pay anything. You should have showed mercy to that other servant, just as I showed mercy to you." The master was very angry and put the servant in prison to be punished until he could pay everything he owed.

'This king did what my heavenly Father will do to you if you do not forgive your brother or sister from your heart'" (Matthew 18:21-35, *NCV*).

## Purpose
Explore the meaning of forgiveness, how to forgive and how often we need to forgive and be forgiven.

## Uncle Arlie's Story
I remember one Christmas when I was 10 or 11 years old. I told my parents that what I wanted most was a new basketball, one without laces. Back in the 1940s, leather basketballs had laces just like footballs today! The temptation was too strong to resist a peek in the closet where my parents hid Christmas gifts. I carefully unwrapped just enough to see what I was getting. I was devastated! It was not the basketball of my dreams, but an inflatable rubber ball. I was upset. When I opened the present on Christmas, I was not happy. My parents knew it. Little did I know at the time that my parents simply couldn't afford a leather basketball. They knew how much I loved basketball so they saved all they could to get me a rubber basketball. Actually, when inflated, the rubber ball became bigger than a normal basketball and made me a better shot because I had to be more accurate getting it through the rim. Much later I told my parents I was sorry for being upset that I didn't get the basketball I wanted. I told them I was thankful for the one they got me because it had

helped me become a long-shot wizard!

Wouldn't it be nice if we would never have to say, "I'm sorry"? We don't live in a perfect world and we are not perfect people. Jesus was the only perfect man to walk on the face of this earth. Learning how to forgive is important for our relationship with God and others.

Discussion

1. What happened to the servant in the story when he did not forgive? What does this mean for us if we don't forgive others?
2. Do you find it easy or hard to say the words "I'm sorry" or "I forgive you"? What makes it easier?
3. How do you feel when you hear the words "You're forgiven"?
4. What does it mean to really forgive someone the way God has forgiven you? How many times should you forgive someone?
5. What can you do in your family to make it easier to say, "I'm sorry" and to grant forgiveness to one another?

Sentence Prayer

Have each member complete each sentence:

> Lord, I thank You for . . .
> Lord, please forgive me for . . .
> Lord, help me to be more . . .
>
> Close with the Lord's Prayer.

# Family Devotion #5

## Devotional Focus
"And do not cause us to be tempted, but save us from the Evil One" (Matthew 6:13, *NCV*).

## Scripture Reading
"We know that the law is spiritual, but I am not spiritual since sin rules me as if I were its slave. I do not understand the things I do. I do not do what I want to do, and I do the things I hate. And if I do not want to do the hated things I do, that means I agree that the law is good. But I am not really the one who is doing these hated things; it is sin living in me that does them. Yes, I know that nothing good lives in me—I mean nothing good lives in the part of me that is earthly and sinful. I want to do the things that are good, but I do not do them. I do not do the good things I want to do, but I do the bad things I do not want to do. So if I do things I do not want to do, then I am not the one doing them. It is sin living in me that does those things.

"So I have learned this rule: When I want to do good, evil is there with me. In my mind, I am happy with God's law. But I see another law working in my body, which makes war against the law that my mind accepts. That other law working in my body is the law of sin, and it makes me its prisoner. What a miserable man I am! Who will save me from this body that brings me death? I thank

God for saving me through Jesus Christ our Lord! So in my mind I am a slave to God's law, but in my sinful self I am a slave to the law of sin" (Romans 7:14-25, *NCV*).

## Purpose
Realize that we are in a spiritual warfare and we also fight against our own evil desires, which can destroy us by pulling us away from our Lord Jesus Christ. Encouragement to have confidence that God who is in us is greater than the evil one who is in the world.

## Uncle Arlie's Story
One hot day on the farm in southern Minnesota, when I was 11 years old, I was helping my father clean the chicken coop. Mother was in the house baking bread. My uncle, an old stonecutter from Sweden, was living with us. While he was handy to have around, he did like chewing his Copenhagen tobacco ("snuff" he called it). My dad had told me that I was not to chew tobacco, and my uncle even said the same thing to me. But I was tempted. I really wanted to try it even though I knew I wasn't supposed to. Without my uncle being aware, I gathered up some of his empty cans of snuff and scraped out enough tobacco to put behind my upper lip just like my uncle did. I didn't want anyone to see me, so I went behind the barn. All of a sudden my dad showed up and said, "Hurry up, and get out here! Pastor Danielson is coming up the

driveway." Well, not wanting to get caught and be punished by my dad, I swallowed the wad of tobacco that was in my mouth. I should have taken the punishment from my dad, because I immediately got sick. I sat down in the hot sun and leaned against the barn, hoping I would die. I never did see the pastor that day, but I learned a great lesson: When you are tempted to do something you know you shouldn't, don't do it.

## Discussion

1. When was a time you were tempted to do something wrong? What happened?
2. What helps you keep from doing wrong?
3. How does God "save us from the Evil One"? What can you do to stay away from the Evil One?
4. Have you ever felt like Paul describes in the Romans passage? What are the two "laws" he talks about at work in him? Why do you think they war against each other?
5. What can we do in our family to help each other resist the temptation to do wrong?

## Circle Prayer

Sit or stand in a circle and join hands. Have the tallest person in the circle begin the prayer time and when finished, he or she squeezes the hand of the next person, who prays. Continue around the circle until everyone has prayed, and then end with the Lord's Prayer.

# Family Devotion #6

## Devotional Focus
"The kingdom, the power, and the glory are yours forever. Amen" (Matthew 6:13, *NCV*).

## Scripture Reading
"Don't think that I have come to destroy the law of Moses or the teaching of the prophets. I have not come to destroy them but to bring about what they said. I tell you the truth, nothing will disappear from the law until heaven and earth are gone. Not even the smallest letter or the smallest part of a letter will be lost until everything has happened. Whoever refuses to obey any command and teaches other people not to obey that command will be the least important in the kingdom of heaven. But whoever obeys the commands and teaches other people to obey them will be great in the kingdom of heaven. I tell you that if you are no more obedient than the teachers of the law and the Pharisees, you will never enter the kingdom of heaven" (Matthew 5:17-20, *NCV*).

## Purpose
To know the what, where, when and how of God's kingdom.

## Uncle Arlie's Story
I have been told I have a rare combination of diseases that are terminal. I would like to live a normal,

healthy life. I would like to see my eight-year-old granddaughter graduate from high school, college, and maybe see her get married some day. But then, God's eternal kingdom beckons us all, and only God knows how long all of us have to live on this side of eternity. I have walked with the Lord most of my life and have been the recipient of His many gifts in spite of the many times I have failed Him, and even strayed from Him. God has understood my human weakness, and He continues to guide and lead me as I strive to live within the "now" of His kingdom.

I fully believe with all of my heart that we live daily in God's kingdom. Our sin prevents us from completely experiencing the fullness of it, but we get a foretaste here on earth of the feast to come. God's kingdom is found in the peace from God that passes all understanding no matter what difficulties we face. God's kingdom is the feeling that comes from being forgiven by someone we have wronged. God's kingdom is the unconditional love we receive from family and friends. God's kingdom is the hope we have no matter what the world looks like. Please don't feel sorry for me, because we are all born with a terminal condition. Our time on earth will come to an end, and that is when our full life with Christ will begin! I'm reminded of the words to a Christian song that talked about people wondering why you are dancing while your days are few, and it's because you know you are a day closer to Jesus. So where is God's kingdom? Is it somewhere out there toward where we are going? Or is the kingdom of God here and now in the life we are living day after day? Look around you and see God's kingdom now, even as you strive toward what will be for all eternity.

Discussion

1. Who did Jesus say would be great in the kingdom of God?
2. Who rules in God's kingdom? What ways can you give glory and honor to the King in that kingdom?
3. How have you experienced God's kingdom in your life here on earth? Who do you know that is part of that kingdom already? How do they live as children of the King?
4. What is something you look forward to seeing, experiencing, in God's kingdom in heaven?
5. What is one thing we can do in our home to bring God's kingdom closer to our family?
6. Who do you know who needs to become part of God's kingdom? Are you willing to commit to praying them into the kingdom?

Prayer Time

Pray the Lord's Prayer by having each person pray a portion of the prayer and complete the open statement at the end, putting the phrase in their own words.

- *Our Father in heaven, may your name always be kept holy.* In my own words, Lord, this means . . .

- *May your kingdom come and what you want be done, here on earth as it is in heaven.* In my own words, Lord, this means . . .

- *Give us the food we need for each day.* In my own words, Lord, this means . . .

- *Forgive us for our sins, just as we have forgiven those who sinned against us.* In my own words, Lord, this means . . .

- *And do not cause us to be tempted, but save us from the Evil One.* In my own words, Lord, this means . . .

- *The kingdom, the power, and the glory are yours forever. Amen.* In my own words, Lord, this means . . .

# Final Words

It has truly been my privilege to take this journey with you through family devotions. I remain convinced that the Christian way of life is more about being devotional than simply doing devotions. Now don't get me wrong, doing devotions on a regular basis will bring you closer to God and each other. Imagine what would happen when you engage in devotional conversations all the time! Hopefully, we have dispelled some myths and provided some tools so you can be a devotional family that connects with God in all circumstances.

A variety of research indicates that current Christian teenagers are going to walk away from the faith when they are young adults. Why? Why are teenagers who are involved in church programs walking away from the faith when they are young adults? The number-one reason cited by numerous sources is hypocrisy. These teenagers believe Christianity is a bunch of hypocrisy, and that's due to the fact that while they were involved in church they were raised in a home environment where there was little or no faith-talk, prayer or devotions. In other words, they were raised in an environment where faith was something you did at church and not at home. When these teenagers become young adults who can choose for themselves, they choose to walk away from the faith, saying, in essence, "If that's what Christianity is, something you only do at church, then I don't want anything to do with it."

I know you do not want your children to walk away from the faith when they are young adults. I know you want them to have the type of faith that will stick with them for life and will positively influence the decisions they make. That is why devotional living is so important. We cannot be "at church only" Christians. We also cannot rely on the experts at church to do it for us. We need to be actively and continually engaged Christ-followers who live devotionally with our children. That, my friends, will lead them to have a faith that sticks with them for life.

Let me close by praying this blessing over you: May the Lord bless you and keep you. May the Lord make His face shine on you and be gracious to you. May the Lord continue to look upon you with favor and give you peace as you live devotionally and engage in family devotions. In the name of the Father, and the Son and the Holy Spirit. Amen.

# Acknowledgments

I first want to give credit to our Lord and Savior Jesus Christ who is the One who deserves all the acknowledgment for anything that is gained through this resource. God is my inspiration; I am simply an instrument through which He has chosen to work. I also want to thank my editor, Jean Lawson, as well as the faithful team of people at Gospel Light who have wholeheartedly supported this series of resources and Faith@Home movement, even before it was a movement. And finally, I want to thank my wife, Maria, and my daughter, Malyn, who are on this devotional journey with me. Thank you for your faithfulness, unconditional love and commitment.

# MARK A. HOLMEN

To find out more about Mark Holmen's speaking
engagements and to learn more about the
Faith@Home movement, visit faithathome.com.
Mark is available to speak to parents and church
leaders about how to be a faith-at-home focused
individual, family and church. For more information,
please contact Mark at mark@faithathome.com.